First World War
and Army of Occupation
War Diary
France, Belgium and Germany

59 DIVISION
176 Infantry Brigade
Prince of Wales's (North Staffordshire Regiment)
2/5th Battalion
1 January 1916 - 29 February 1916

WO95/3021/2

Published by

The Naval & Military Press Ltd

Unit 10 Ridgewood Industrial Park,

Uckfield, East Sussex,

TN22 5QE England

Tel: +44 (0) 1825 749494

www.naval-military-press.com

www.nmarchive.com

This diary has been reprinted in facsimile from the original. Any imperfections are inevitably reproduced and the quality may fall short of modern type and cartographic standards.

© **Crown Copyright**
Images reproduced by permission of The National Archives, London, England, 2015.

Contents

Document type	Place/Title	Date From	Date To
Heading	WO95/3021/2		
Heading	War Diary of 2/5 North Stafford Regt From Jan 1st 1916 To Jan 31st 1916 Volume 1		
War Diary	St Albans	01/01/1916	31/01/1916
Miscellaneous	Appendix 1 Out Break of Scabies Reports by Medical Officers 2/5 North Staffs Regt Jany 1916		
Miscellaneous	2/5 North Stafford Regt Outbreak Of Scabies		
Miscellaneous	Appendix 2 Air Raids-Jan 28/16		
Miscellaneous	The Officer Commanding, 2/5 North Stafford Regiment	28/01/1916	28/01/1916
Miscellaneous	A Form Messages And Signals		
Miscellaneous	Appendix 3 Air Raid Jan 31/16		
Miscellaneous	A Form Messages And Signals		
Heading	War Diary of 2/5 North Stafford Regt (T.F) From Feby 1st 1916 To Feby 29th 1916 Volume 1		
War Diary	St Albans	01/02/1916	29/02/1916
Miscellaneous	A Form Messages And Signals		

weerslagen 1/20021/9

CONFIDENTIAL

WAR DIARY

of

2/5 NORTH STAFFORD REGT

from Jan 1st 1916   to Jan 31st 1916

VOLUME 1

Arthur J Hau. Lt Col
comdg 2/5 NORTH STAFFS Regt

Army Form C. 2118.

WAR DIARY
INTELLIGENCE SUMMARY
(Erase heading not required.)

Instructions regarding War Diaries and Intelligence Summaries are contained in F.S. Regs., Part II. and the Staff Manual respectively. Title pages will be prepared in manuscript.

Hour, Date, Place	Summary of Events and Information	Remarks and references to Appendices
1.1.16. St. ALBANS.	Strength of Battn. Officers 27 Other Ranks 629	
2.1.16 "	Nil.	
3.1.16 "	Nil.	
4.1.16 "	Capt. H.E. MacGowan transferred to 3/5 South Staffs. Regt.	
5.1.16 "	Nil.	see Appx. 1
6.1.16 "	Bunners Special Training for A & B Coy Commanders	
7.1.16 "	Outbreak of Scabies	
8.1.16 "	Nil	
9.1.16 "	Nil	
10.1.16 "	Nil	
11.1.16 "	Nil	
12.1.16 "	Nil	
13.1.16 "	Battn. to be made up to 850 other ranks from Grps 2.3.4.5. Army Reserve	
14.1.16 "	Nil	
15.1.16 "	2/Lts H.R. Cunwick 2/Lt. T.R. Malkin & 2/Lt. A. Benson - transferred to Provisional Brigade. Tendring. Essex - unfit for foreign Service.	
16.1.16 "		
17.1.16 "	Nil	

Army Form C. 2118.

WAR DIARY
OR
INTELLIGENCE SUMMARY.
(Erase heading not required.)

Instructions regarding War Diaries and Intelligence Summaries are contained in F.S. Regs., Part II. and the Staff Manual respectively. Title pages will be prepared in manuscript.

Hour, Date, Place	Summary of Events and Information	Remarks and references to Appendices
18.1.16. ST. ALBANS.	Nil	pcs
19.1.16 "	Nil	pcs
20.1.16 "	Nil	pcs
21.1.16 "	Nil	pcs
22.1.16 "	Nil	pcs
23.1.16 "	Nil	pcs
24.1.16 "	40 Reservists joins from Administrative Unit	pcs
25.1.16 "	Nil	pcs
26.1.16 "	33 Reservists joined from Administrative Unit	pcs
27.1.16 "	40 Reservists joined from Administrative Unit	pcs
28.1.16 "	9.45p warning from Brigade HQrs - Zeppelin Raid on EAST COAST - not sighted by this unit.	App: 2.
29.1.16 "	Nil.	pcs
30.1.16 "	Nil.	pcs
31.1.16 "	7.30p MESSAGE from Bgde HQrs - Air Raid on EAST COAST - no air raid by this unit.	App. 3.

Anthony Maw Lt Col
First 7th Middlesex Regt

Appendix 1

Outbreak of SCABIES

– Reports by Medical Officers.

7/5 North Staffs Regt.

Jany: 1916.

9/25 NORTH STAFFORD REGT

Outbreak of Scabies

Jan 7/16	3 Cases
" 13/16	2 "
" 20/16	25 "
" 27/16	9 "
" 29/16	5 "
" 30/16	1 "
" 31/16	1 "

APPENDIX 2

AIR RAIDS - June 28/16

Message / Morning letters from

176: Infantry Brigade

June 28/16.

APPENDIX 2.

AIR RAIDS

The Officer Commanding,
   2/5 North Stafford Regiment.

   The annexed is forwarded for your information, and attention; please be prepared act as detailed in para (1) of Standing Orders in case of an Air Raid; on receipt of further orders; no action has at present been taken throughout the country.

C. O. Langley

ST. ALBANS.   Captain. Brigade Major.
28...1..16.   176th Infantry Brigade.

"A" Form.
Army Form C. 2121.

MESSAGES AND SIGNALS.

No. of Message _____

Prefix ____ Code ____ m.	Words	Charge	This message is on a/c of:	Recd. at ____ m.
Office of Origin and Service Instructions	Sent			Date ____
	At ____ m.		____ Service.	From ____
	To ____			By ____
	By ____		(Signature of "Franking Officer.")	

TO 2/6 L Staffs R

| Sender's Number. | Day of Month. | In reply to Number | AAA |
| 9/5/ | 28d | | |

Phone message received from Divisional H.Q. as follows — 3rd Army report Zeppelin raid but sh'd say have not come so far as ST ALBANS aaa They are keeping more to the East coast aaa message ends aaa

From 176
Place
Time 8.45 pm

The above may be forwarded as now corrected.   (Z).   C.O. 2/6 ____

Censor.   Signature of Addressor or person authorised to telegraph in his name.

* This line should be erased if not required.

1/6 North Staffs Regt

APPENDIX 3

A/c Raid from 31/1/16.

4 Messages from
1/6: Infantry Bgde.

"A" Form.
MESSAGES AND SIGNALS. Army Form C. 2121.

Prefix	Code	m.	Words	Charge	This message is on a/c of:	Recd. at	m.
Office of Origin and Service Instructions.		Sent			Service.	Date	
		At		m.		From	
		To					
		By			(Signature of "Franking Officer.")	By	

TO { O C 2/5th N. Staffs R

Sender's Number.	Day of Month.	In reply to Number	
*	31/1/16		A A A

The following telephone message just received from Divisional Headquarters on the way 3 Zeppelins on way to Banbridge to London working from on G E all traffic stopped on line aaa. Please act in accordance with air Raid orders at once. Firing parties will be prevented. aaa

From 176 B
Place
Time

"A" Form.
Army Form C. 2121.

MESSAGES AND SIGNALS.

TO: 2/5th N. Staffs R

Day of Month: 31st

AAA

Firing parties will be warned to turn out on receiving further orders; pending such orders they will not be turned out.

From: 176 B
Time: 7.45 pm

176th Inf Bde

CONFIDENTIAL.

WAR DIARY

of.

2/5 NORTH STAFFORD REGT. (TF)

from Feby 1st 1916.   to Feby 29th 1916

Volume 1

Harry Johnson
Major
for Lt Col
(and) 2/5 North Staff Regt

WAR DIARY
OR
INTELLIGENCE SUMMARY
(Erase heading not required.)

2/5 NORTH STAFFORD Regt Army Form C. 2118

Instructions regarding War Diaries and Intelligence Summaries are contained in F.S. Regs., Part II. and the Staff Manual respectively. Title Pages will be prepared in manuscript.

Place	Date	Hour	Summary of Events and Information	Remarks and references to Appendices
St Albans	1.2.16	—	Strength of Battn. Officers 34. Other Ranks 729	V.C.A
"	2.2.16	12 noon	Inspection of Battn. on Route March by Lt. Gen Sir A. CODRINGTON – Comg. III rd Army.	V.C.A
"	3.2.16		32 Reservists joined from Administrative Centre.	V.C.A
"	5.2.16		21 Reservists joined from Administrative Centre.	V.C.A
"	11.2.16		75 Reservists joined from Administrative Centre.	V.C.A
"	11.2.16		Board of Survey on Young Officers	V.C.A
"	12.2.16		Lt. L. ARROWSMITH (enlist for Foreign Service) reports to Headquarters NORTHERN COMMAND.	V.C.A
"	14.2.16		Maj. Genl. A.E. SANDBACH takes over Command of 59 (N.M.) Division from Maj. Genl R.M.R. READE – No 4525	V.C.A
"	16.2.16		Capt. & Q.M. G.H. SWANN relinquishes his commission on account of ill health. a/Sq Major G.F. HARRIS. 9 Jellas Hon Lieut & QM. in this Battalion.	V.C.A
"	16.2.16		Col. L. R. CARLETON D.S.O.; G.S.O.i 59 (NM) Div. takes over Command of the 176 Infantry Brigade from Colonel. H. A. CHANDOS-POLE-GELL	V.C.A
"	17.2.16		23 Reservists from Administrative Centre	V.C.A
"	24.2.16	?	Lecture by Capt. GOULD. R.A.M.C. "Aid to Gas measures for Defence" in the Culver Hall.	V.C.A
"	26.2.16	4 pm	Brigade Officers meeting – "All Leave Stopped" – Battalion confined to Billeting Area.	V.C.A
"	28.2.16	10.30 am	Inspection of Reservists by Maj. Genl. A.E. SANDBACH	V.C.A
"	29.2.16	11 am	The "EMERGENCY MOOR" - the Battalion was ready to move to its entraining station in 2 hours. Lt. Genl Sir A. CODRINGTON. Cmdg III rd Army, inspected the Battn when ready to move.	V.C.A

Harry Johnson
Major & Lt Col
Comdg 2/5th North Staffs Regt.

"A" Form.   Army Form C. 2121.

MESSAGES AND SIGNALS.

TO   OC 2/5 H Sapp R

Day of Month: 3

The following message has been received from Divisional Headquarters

2 Zeppelins at BROXBOURNE in Herts at 7.30 pm aaa Firing parties will turn out

From 176 B
Place
Time 8.15 pm

"A" Form. Army Form C. 2121.

MESSAGES AND SIGNALS.

| TO | 2/5th K. Staff |

Day of Month: 31st

AAA

Firing parties are to be called in but to be prepared to turn out if required

From: 70 B
Place:
Time: 9.35 pm

C.O. Langley Capt
B/O May
76th Inf Bde

www.ingramcontent.com/pod-product-compliance
Lightning Source LLC
Chambersburg PA
CBHW081510160426
43193CB00014B/2646